**Everyday words
used in this book**

the

we

be

me

of

to

she

was

I

**New words
used in this book**

death

place

away

they

smells

fresh

A bad smell fills the hut.
Tom gets up from the bed.

"Nell, get up.
We must get away from this place.
We must set off."

Nell sobs.
"Tom, will we get ill?"

"Not if we get away
from the rats, Nell.
If we get the bug
it will be the end of us.
We must not get sick."

"Let me dress, Tom,
and then we can set off."

It is 1665.
Rats from the ships
live in the mud and muck
in the docks.

The smell is bad.
The Black Death is on the backs
of the rats.

The Black Death kills.

Tom picks up a bag
and they set off.

They run past the docks.
They run past the ships.
They run past the huts
with a red cross on them.
The red cross of death.

They run and run to get away.
Nell trips on the ruts,
but Tom helps.

"Get up, Nell.
We must not stop.
We must not get sick."

Tom and Nell run on
past the bog
and past the pits.

The men had dug the death pits
as the Black Death hit.

The smell of death hit Nell.
She felt sick.

"Can we stop, Tom?
I must stop," gasps Nell.

Tom spots a place to rest.
They sit and rest.

As the sun gets hot,
Tom and Nell get up.

Tom helps Nell up a hill
of grass and moss.

At the top Tom grins.

"This is the place.
It smells fresh.
The rats and the Black Death
will not get us.
We can be well in this place."

"Yes, Tom, we can,"
Nell nods.

Nell did not tell Tom
that she was not well.

She felt hot and sick.

The Language of Birds

Eoin McNamee

Dublin

The Language of Birds
is first published in 1995 by
New Island Books
2 Brookside,
Dundrum Road,
Dublin 14,
Ireland

ISBN 1 874597 18 9

● ● ● ● ● ● ●

New Island Books receives financial assistance from
The Arts Council (An Comhairle Ealaíon)
Dublin, Ireland

The publishers would like to acknowledge the assistance of
The Arts Council of Northern Ireland
in the publication of this title.

Title originated by The Raven Arts Press.
Cover Design by Jon Berkeley,
Typesetting by Graphic Resources,
Printed in Ireland by Colour Books, Ltd.

The Language of Birds

Contents

In memory of
Brendan McNamee
1931 - 1992

Part I

Coalisland

When he brought me to Coalisland snooker hall
He was eleven, just home from boarding school.

He had stammered since the day he found
His parents shot dead in their back lane,

His tongue an inarticulate fist
In the nervous glove of his lips,

But he became fluent on the table;
Intent on the cue he would straddle

It the way I straddled you in the passenger seat,
Your new orange dress above your waist

In a layby at the Long Woman's Grave.

They had parked the car when he found them
And were sitting so quietly it might have been

That her dress had slipped above her hips,
Or that his hand had made a fist in his lap.

Intensive Care

"Queenio, Queenio,
Who's got the ball?"

It reminded me of radar:
A dumbstruck
Ball of light
Hurled through silence.

"I haven't got it
In my pocket."

A far cry
From the bow-swung
Plumbline
The Phoenician invented.

"Queenio, Queenio,
Who's got the ball?"

And a far cry
From your astonished face
When I came upon it
In a hospital bed.

"I haven't got it
In my pocket."

A curious intentness
About you, as if you were taking
Deep soundings
From the heart monitor.

"Queenio, Queenio,
Who's got the ball?"

Its sonic blip
A tennis ball
You lobbed and retrieved
From the wall of your heart

"I haven't got it
In my pocket."

While the nurse keeps half
An eye on the screen
For the one that bounces
Out of reach.

"Queenio, Queenio,
Who's got the ball?"

On Your Back

In your bed
the moist interior stink, a sauce of making
beneath the sheets.
Sweet suckling wormwood, herb of breathing
on your mouth.

Under your belly
an opened muscle, a slack-mouthed, salty
mollusc.

Thigh on thigh, deepfeeding, austere,
on your back.

Greengrocer, London SE 11

On Hayles Street, next to the nettled
Wasteland levelled by a doodlebug

He opens his shop like the bright
Conspiratorial passages of an atlas,

Tucks his sweater into the frayed
Waistband of his demob suit and weighs out

The mapped atrocities of his stock,
Their vegetable complicity.

What news of a cantaloupe?

A cabbage gapes like a famine,
The beet is an injured, mouthless glob.

"Bananas from Nicaragua? You must be joking
Forty pence a frigging pound since United Fruit

Pulled their mob out of Costa Rica."
Well-versed in conspiracies and embargoes

He knows when someone's being punished,
How the stem grips the tomatoes' juicy

Nipple like an electrode,
That the tuberous dead fill the holds

Of ships on the Suez, packed
In boxes with yellow, Egyptian earth.

The Clinic

We filled the cistern
In the yard
With frogspawn in jars

Half-pints,
Pudgy little fists
Yawning half-awake

And making faces.
Their sleepyheads
And immaculate scalps

Brought you back
To the vanilla scoop
In the surgeon's bucket

And you loafing around
In a surgical gown
Until you met the frog

Who gently undid
The tape at your waist
And sat back

On thumbnail-sized
Muddy hunkers
Waiting to be kissed.

The Language of Birds

Weather out of Siberia.
We never expected it
Or the watchful migrants
Unlocked from the Baltic

Frigid birdbrains
Breaking cover across
The map, settling
In Carlingford Lough

Feathered cortex
To feathered cortex.
Poles apart
Their arctic talk

Won't translate.
They'll go in the spring
And they won't apologise
For having left

Next to nothing.
They might come back.
Meanwhile concern yourself
With what little is left,

The fledgling weight,
The stored coldness
That is cogent, worn
Next to the skin.

Amazon

In the attic of our first house
We found a wall
Where American pilots, billets
From Cranfield aerodrome
Pinned their pin-ups
And wrote their names.

Squadron upon squadron
Of heavy-engined bombers
Bringing the house down
All over Europe,

Though sometimes they overshot
On the way back, coming
Unstuck against a mountain,
One that dropped short
Left a barnacled engine
On the beach near Kitty's road.

They kept to themselves
And when they went away
No-one was jilted
Or left holding the baby.

Underneath 'Jake, Flatbush
Avenue, Brooklyn'
A yellowing, pin-up
Betty Grable bares
As much breast as she dares
And cocks her hips across the Atlantic.

Guernica

You wrote to tell me how
You played the back end
Of a mechanical horse
In a piece based
On Picasso's *Guernica*
Which was well-received
At the Belfast Theatre Festival.

In earlier letters you played
The back ends of horses
Dying in the mud at Verdun,
Choking on napalm in Vietnam,
Succumbing to the heat of the sun
At Midway and Hiroshima.

1972
And a moment of abandon
When you played the back end
Of a burned-out bus on the Ormeau Road.

But mainly you stick to horses
Because for every Guernica
There is always someone
Playing the back end of a horse
The way there's always someone
Flying the back end of a Stuka.

Oppenheimer's Dream

While we're scouring Lady Dixon's Park.
for the pointed skullcap of psilocybin

its chess bishop's head.

Oppenheimer's asleep and dreaming
designer mushrooms, chanterelles.

Emigrants

My brother went to Australia for the summer
To stay with an uncle on my mother's side
And wrote back to say how odd it was
To find a Quinn in the Antipodes.

I looked at the three uncles
Who stayed in Mourne, a gaunt triptych
Of hooked noses and bony laughter
Unimaginable on Bondi beach

But not difficult to locate
In the hinterland, artifacts
Of a forgotten race, carved in stone
Under a lizard's adhesive talon.

Folk Museum

The loom's skilled
Arm dips in unison
With my grandfather's head

As he bends to collect
A retted and bleached
Exhibit of linen.

Over there is a boat
Winched from our oily
Scrap of water

To take its place
In a working catalogue
Of lived emblems.

The mechanical loom
Recites the history
Of its invention.

The fishing boat
Lowers its nets
To an imagined depth

To fill its hold
With tamarinds,
Sweet potato.

Ambre Solaire

It's not the slaughter
of the keg bomb I'm after
or the informer

shot dead and lagged
in a black plastic binbag

I'm looking for vowels
liquid as Camlough
ambre solaire

or any other improbable gel
of ditchwater and red diesel

to take the skelped grin
from the faces of children
at the Border Inn

waiting for the Newry bus
that won't come soon enough.

After The Riot

We could not put it out of our minds.
Even afterwards, drinking Bushmills
At your kitchen table
Our soft political talk
Looked over its shoulder

At riot police and plate glass
That collapsed into the street
While we, knowing we were known,
Put our heads down
And ran with the rest.

We could not forget it
Or remember if it was fear
That got my arm
Around your shoulder
For the first time in years.

Indians

"Cold as a witches tit"
A draught that would clean corn
Blows down the avenues
Off the stormy Hudson.

I too much prefer it seems
The voices of my own land,
To eat off oilcloth as it were-
But there's not much I can do

Unless, when I see a voice fumbling
In its bag for a lipstick tissue,
I take flight into
The skies of New Amsterdam

Where Indian fires burn dull ochre
Among the sparse pines below,
Where Indians drink a rare, chilled milk
And do not prosper.

The Heifer

The day she left Mourne,
Its pungent, brackish
Sheughs and bents
Her tongue became a kept orchard,
Trimmed and neatly ditched

Until, thirty years after,
The day when a heifer burst
Through whins onto the road.
An empty purse of veal
Flapped between its legs,

Its startled hooves clipped
A dialect of loanings
And bicycle rides to Mass
That she understood
So that she cried

"Cap thon heifer"
I did as she said
And stopped it
In its tracks.
Head-down language
Stood beyond us,

Skittering, not quite tame.

Elms

The elms are dead here,
Each twig exact,
Equivalent to itself.

Dry lightening,
Volts up there,
A taste of railway

Sidings in the air;
Unlit terminals.
A woman naked in Stern

Holds her thighs apart
As if they hurt her.
Sometimes it's just

Bliss. Men stare.
The snake in the cellar
Articulates his skin

Among the milk cartons.
The mosquito is sunk
Millimetres deep.

There is no sequel.
There is no relief.

Part II

Terminal

There was an X-ray machine in the shoeshop.
You put your feet in. It showed the bones,
The allotted detail of ankle, heel, toes.

When he photographed us it was the negative
That appealed; some mystery acoustic produced
The white hair, the klan eyes, the black smiles

Or the specialist holding up the chest plate
Pointing with a biro to this and that.
The shadow concealed in the slatted bivouac.

Soft Going

Onscreen
Through the fog at Sandown
The fence rails gleam
White, exalted, eerie.

Moody dusk.
What does the horse love?
Soft going.
Holding close to the rail.

Men's hearts that force
Loneliness upon it.
A year after his death
I came across the yellow slips

Hughes Turf accountant.
Yankees, trebles -
A dialect at risk
From tales of the fallen.

It is Winter there,
At Epsom, at ghostly Sandown
And the horses
Verify it.

His Glasses

They're in the hinged cardboard box,
The frames of the weighty black
X-ray specs he wore with cinematic
Effect in the wedding photograph where
His stony grin tells you what to expect.

They gave him the look of a dreamy
Smalltown murderer- McGladdery perhaps
Who saw Pearl Gambol's lovely face
Float up from the cistern like
A photograph from a photographer's bath

New Cortina, 1969

It was there that morning when we went out
Its cold and abstract mass
Just as we had envisaged it.

We had known it was coming all that night,
Noiseless as an airship, with instruments
To measure the miles it covered aloft.

We found him still frozen in the driver's seat
His hair was stiff with frost and his eyes
Were fixed on a perplexing dream of height.

His Death

When it came he offered his paralysed arms
They were frosty, limp, delinquent
He offered his ancestors and their starry outlands
He offered his troubled sleep it might be useful
To death
He offered memories of cold howling sex
He offered his sons.
He offered tax-free cash
He offered his lungs
He said he was the loneliest man on earth

Pneumonia

Monaghan street 1938. We know that
He read the Hotspur underneath the bedclothes
And that when he was finished
The world seemed more ruthless than before.

We know that night there was a warehouse fire
And that he climbed the roof to watch
Half-dressed, frail enough, the night rigged
In lethal air, a galactic chill
Of solitude and disbelief.

It was the coldest February for years
And his lungs filled with clear fluid.
Each day his brother came to the Fever Ward
To tell him stories of unbelievable cold.